ShowTime® Piano

Christmas

Level 2A

Elementary Playing

This book belongs to: _____

Arranged by

Nancy and Randall Faber

Production Coordinator: Jon Ophoff
Design and Illustration: Terpstra Design, San Francisco
Engraving: Dovetree Productions, Inc.

FABER
PIANO ADVENTURES®
3042 Creek Drive
Ann Arbor, Michigan 48108

A NOTE TO TEACHERS

ShowTime® Piano Christmas is a collection of well-loved Christmas songs that includes traditional carols as well as seasonal favorites. The pieces are arranged specifically to provide a smooth transition for the student between Level 1 and Level 2. For this reason, the book is graded 2A.

At the *ShowTime®* level, the student begins to move out of a 5-finger position. A circled finger number is used to alert the student to a change of hand position. Melodies are harmonized simply, using single notes or harmonic intervals.

ShowTime® Piano Christmas is part of the *ShowTime® Piano* series. "ShowTime" designates Level 2A of the *PreTime®* to *BigTime® Piano Supplementary Library* arranged by Faber and Faber.

Following are the levels of the supplementary library, which lead from *PreTime®* to *BigTime®*.

PreTime® Piano	(Primer Level)
PlayTime® Piano	(Level 1)
ShowTime® Piano	(Level 2A)
ChordTime® Piano	(Level 2B)
FunTime® Piano	(Level 3A–3B)
BigTime® Piano	(Level 4)

Each level offers books in a variety of styles, making it possible for the teacher to offer stimulating material for every student. For a complimentary detailed listing, e-mail faber@pianoadventures.com or write us at the mailing address below.

Visit **www.PianoAdventures.com**.

Helpful Hints:

1. Rhythmic continuity can be improved by having the student tap the piece, hands together. (Use the palm or fingertips on the closed fallboard or lap.)

2. Singing the words to **ShowTime® Christmas** can add to the enjoyment and helps the student grasp phrasing and rhythm.

3. Key signatures are not used until late in the *ShowTime®* level. Where key signatures are used, one-octave scales (hands alone) can help orient the student to the piece.

4. As a special project, the student may wish to record his or her favorite Christmas songs. This can be used as memorable Christmas gifts to parents or grandparents.

ISBN 978-1-61677-037-2

TABLE OF CONTENTS

Must Be Santa

Words and Music by
HAL MOORE and BILL FREDRICKS

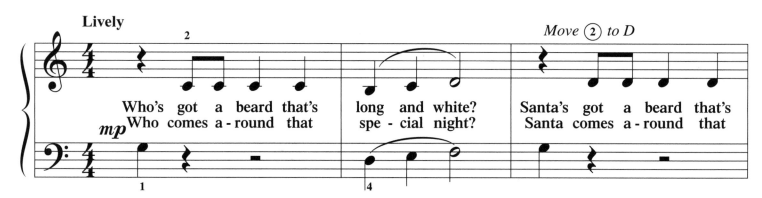

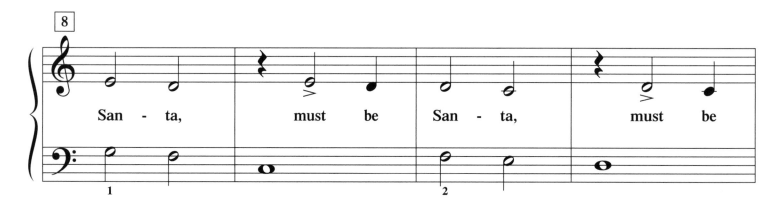

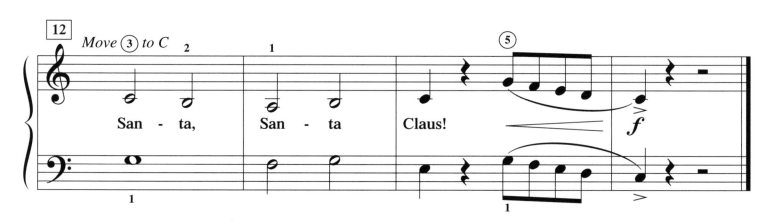

God Bless All

TRADITIONAL

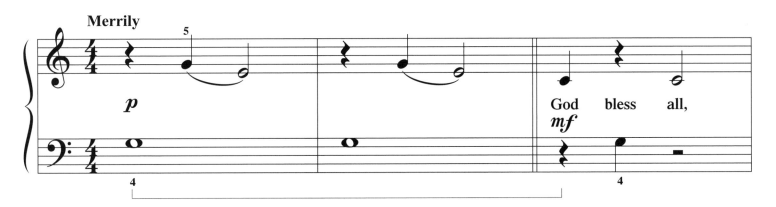

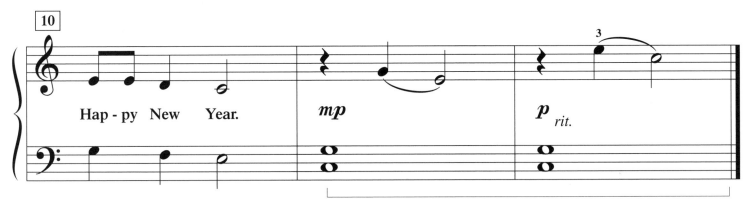

FF1037

Up On the Housetop

Words and Music by
BENJAMIN R. HANBY

Playfully

Both hands in the highest octave on the piano -

a tempo

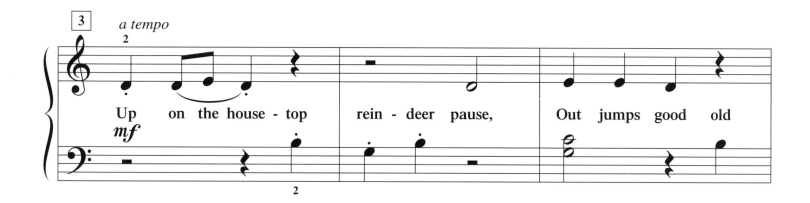

Up on the house-top rein-deer pause, Out jumps good old

San - ta Claus. Down through the chim - ney with lots of toys,

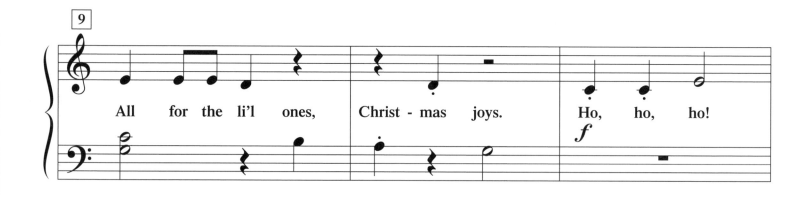

All for the li'l ones, Christ - mas joys. Ho, ho, ho!

Who would-n't go! Ho, ho, ho! Who would-n't go!_____

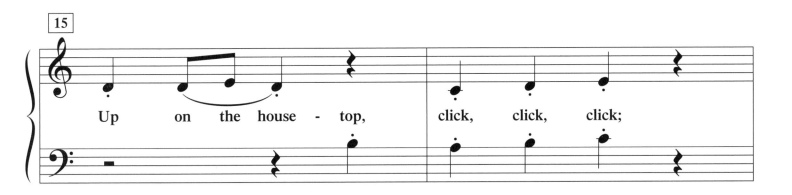

Up on the house - top, click, click, click;

Down through the chim - ney with good St. Nick! *mf*

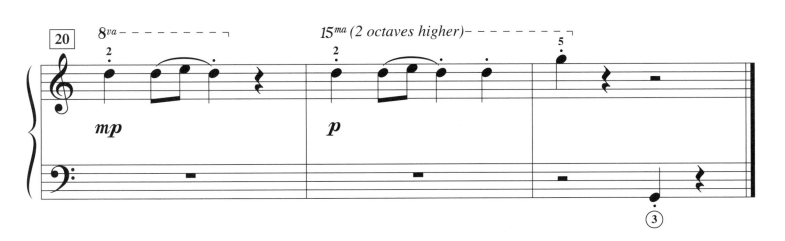

8va - - - - - - -   *15ma (2 octaves higher)- - - - - - - -*

mp   *p*

It Came Upon the Midnight Clear

By E.H. SEARS and R.S. WILLIS

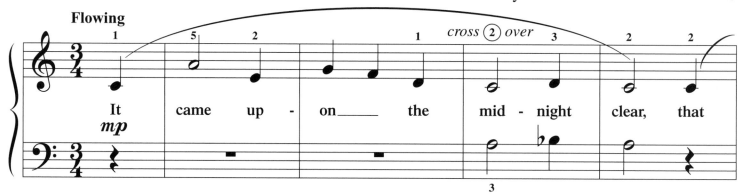

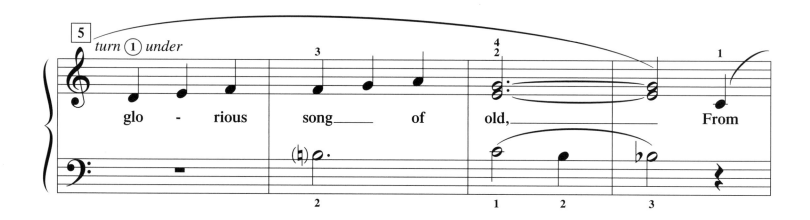

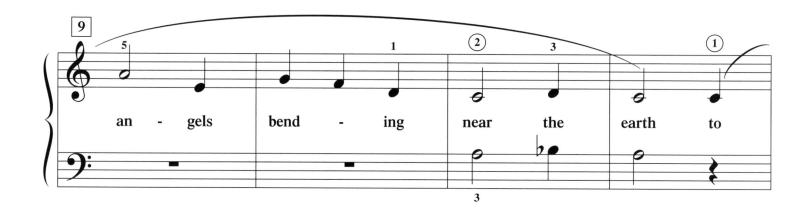

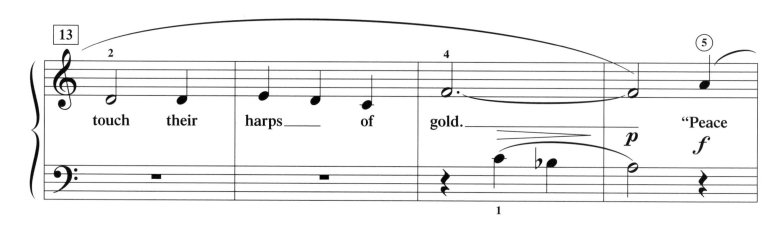

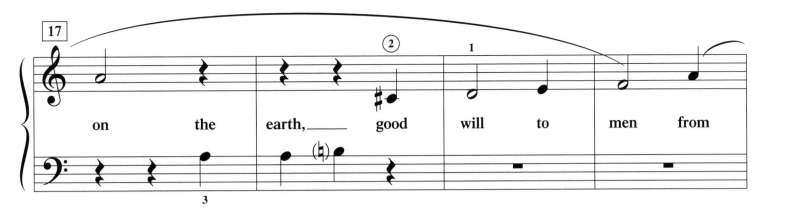

on the earth,_____ good will to men from

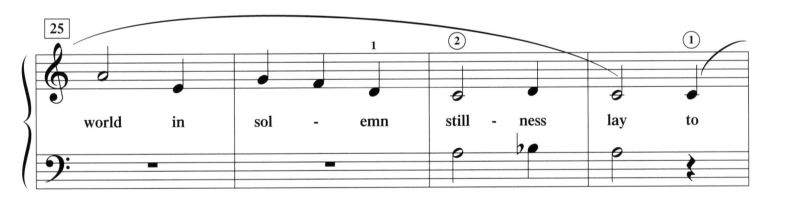

Heav - en's all gra - cious King!" The

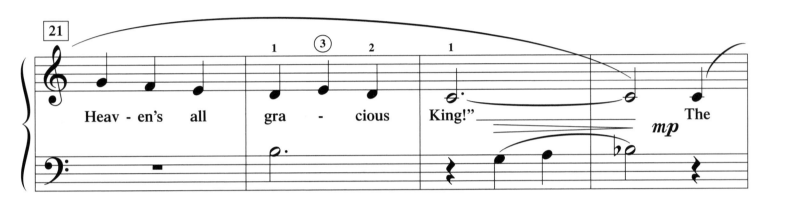

world in sol - emn still - ness lay to

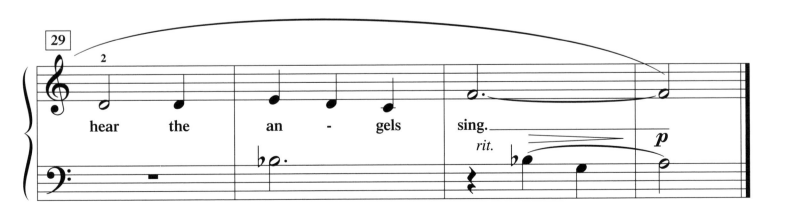

hear the an - gels sing._____

Frosty the Snowman

Words and Music by
STEVE NELSON and JACK ROLLINS

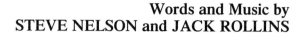

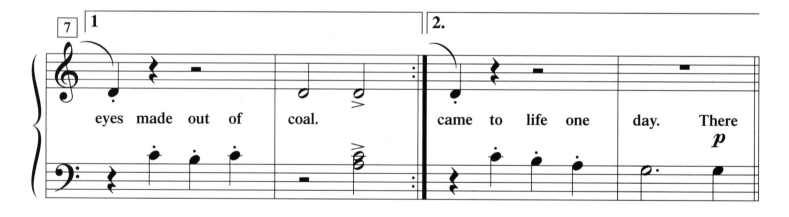

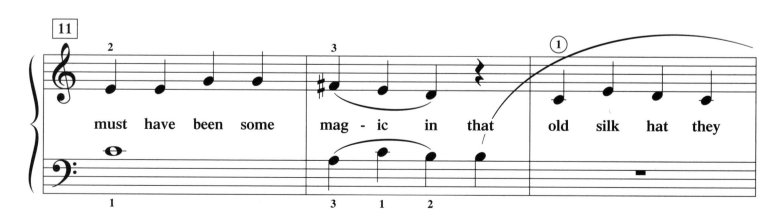

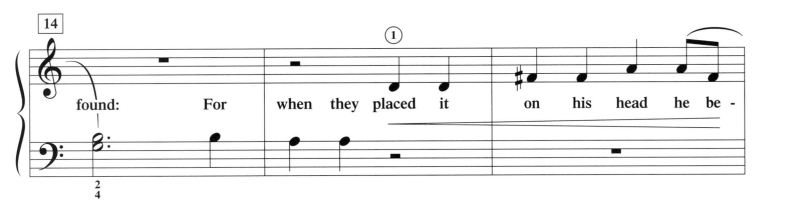

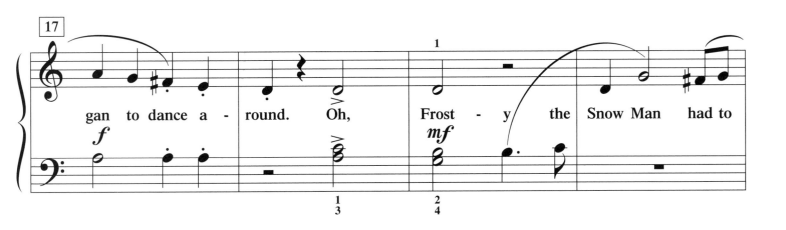

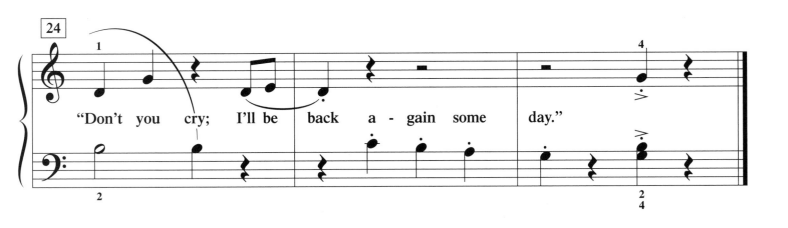

Angels We Have Heard on High

TRADITIONAL

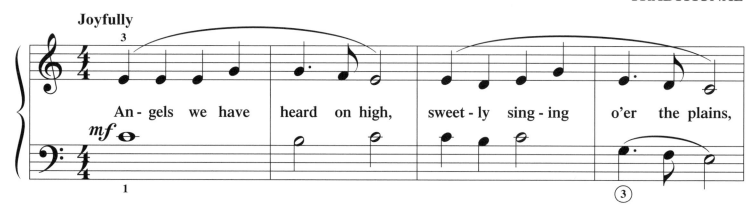

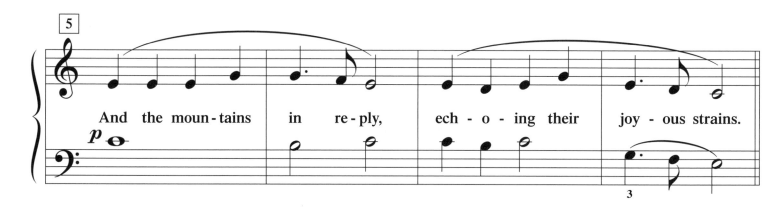

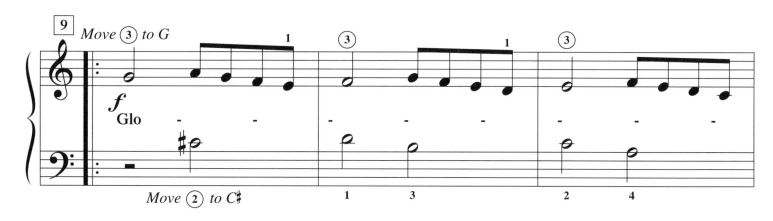

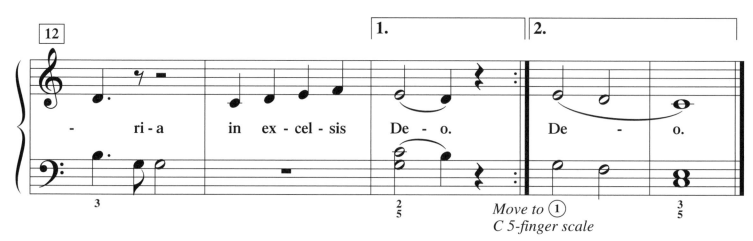

Silent Night

Words by JOSEPH MOHR

Music by FRANZ GRÜBER

FF1037

We Three Kings of Orient Are

Words and Music by
J.H. HOPKINS, Jr.

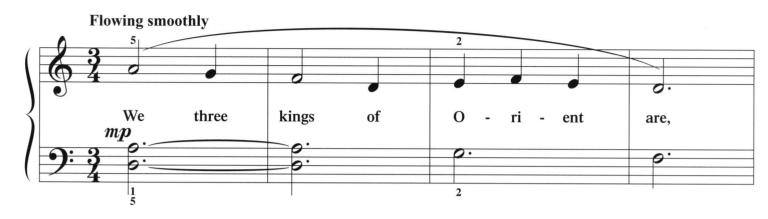

We three kings of O - ri - ent are,

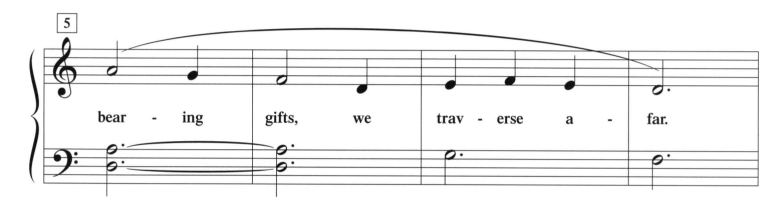

bear - ing gifts, we trav - erse a - far.

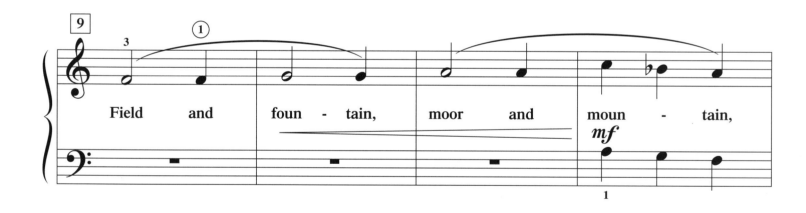

Field and foun - tain, moor and moun - tain,

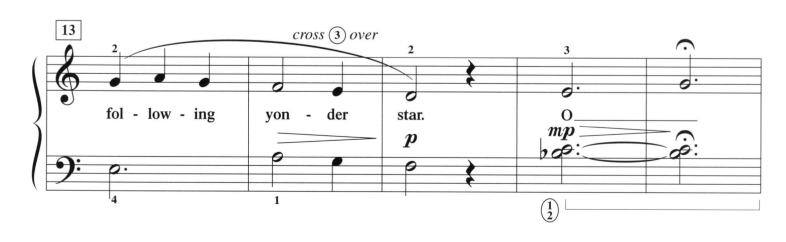

fol - low - ing yon - der star.   O

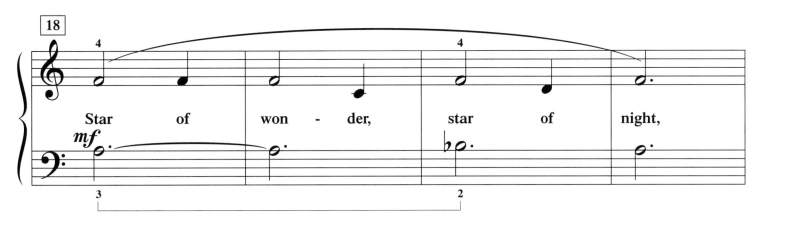

Star of won - der, star of night,

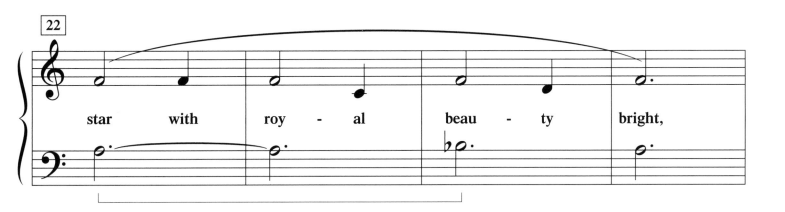

star with roy - al beau - ty bright,

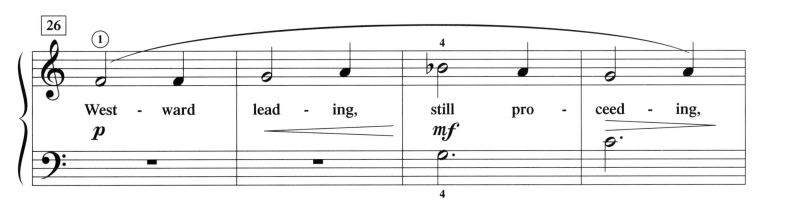

West - ward lead - ing, still pro - ceed - ing,

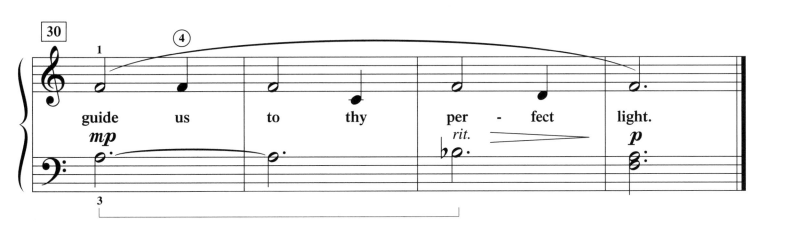

guide us to thy per - fect light.

The Little Drummer Boy

Words and Music by
KATHERINE DAVIS, HENRY ONORATI, and
HARRY SIMEONE

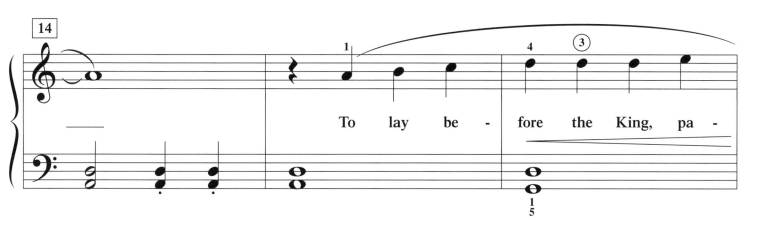

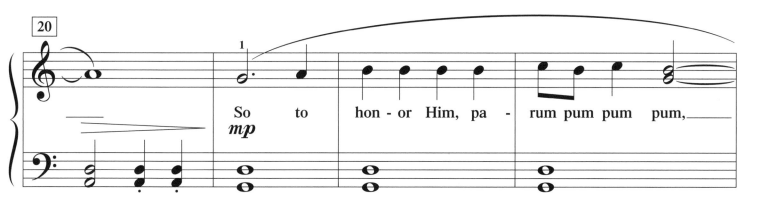

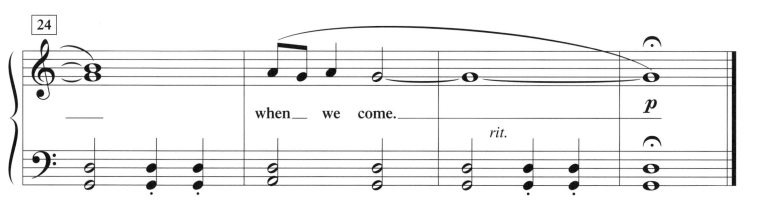

Santa Claus Is Comin' to Town

Words by HAVEN GILLESPIE

Music by J. FRED COOTS

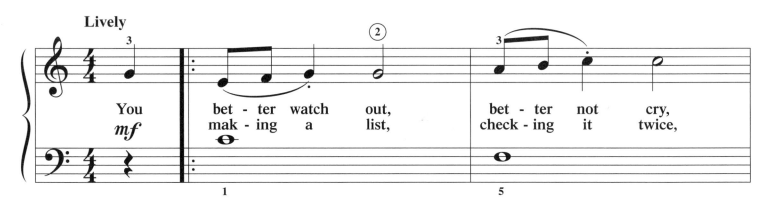

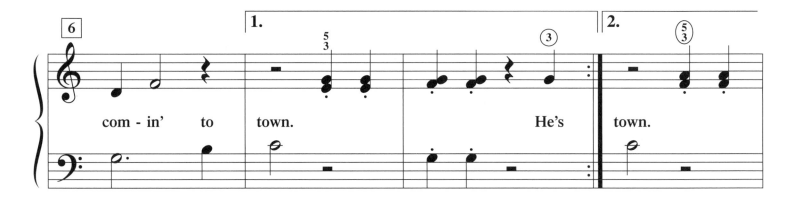

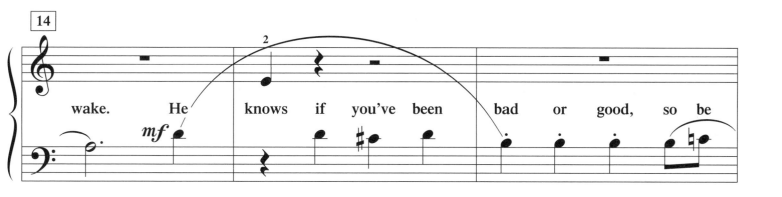

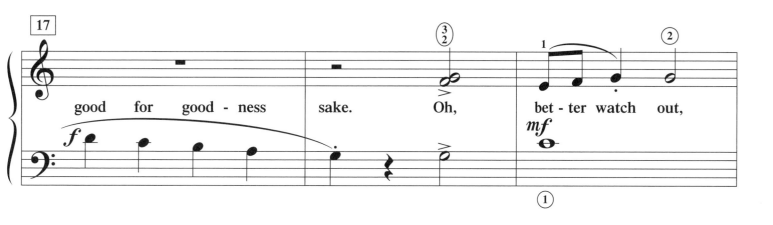

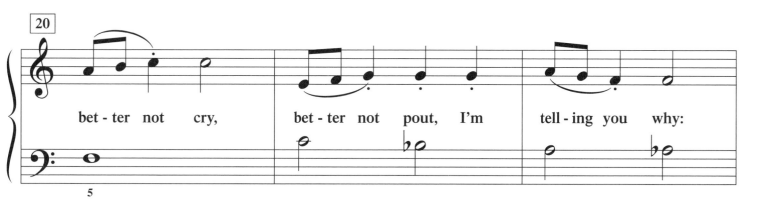

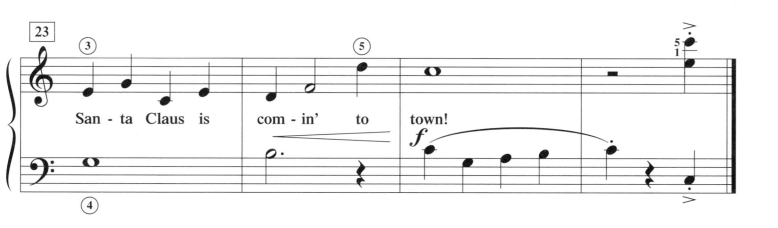

Coventry Carol

TRADITIONAL ENGLISH CAROL

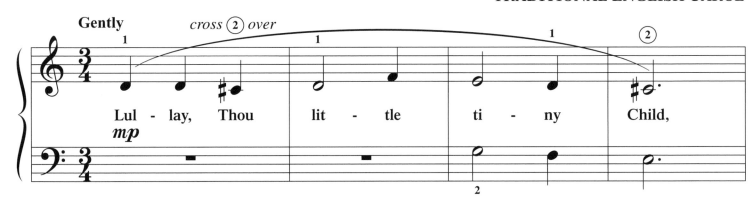

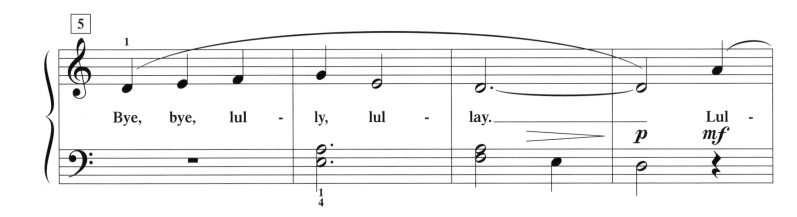

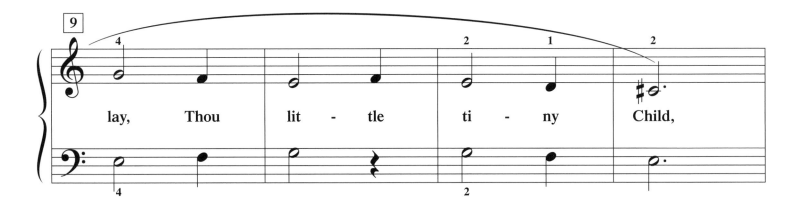

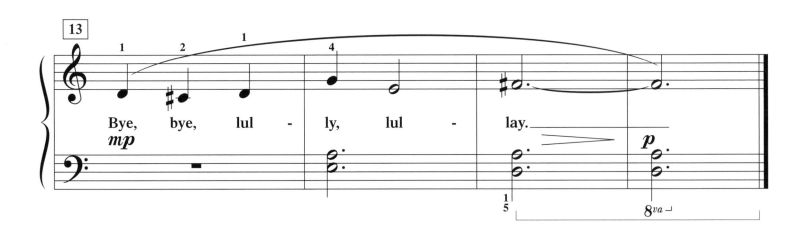

Ding, Dong Merrily on High

FRENCH DANCE

Lyrics under the staves:

Ding, dong, mer-ri-ly on high, the Christ-mas bells are ring-ing;

Ding, dong, joy-ous-ly re-ply, the an-gels all a-sing-ing.

Glo - - - - - - - - - -

- - - - - - cresc. -

-ri - a, Ho - san - na in ex - cel - sis.

Little Elf's Christmas

Lyric by JENNIFER MacLEAN

Music by NANCY FABER

"I'm sup-posed to make the toys," thought the lit - tle elf. "The

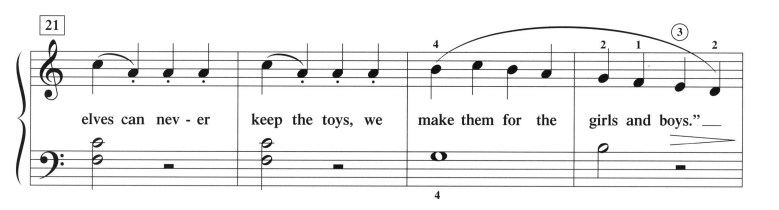

elves can nev - er keep the toys, we make them for the girls and boys."

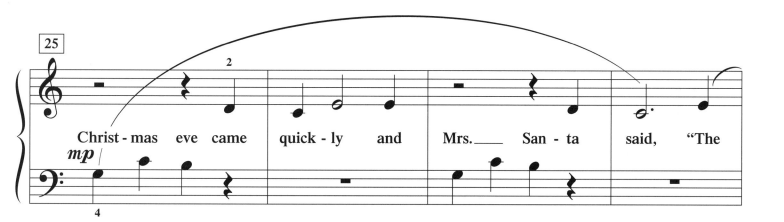

Christ - mas eve came quick - ly and Mrs. San - ta said, "The

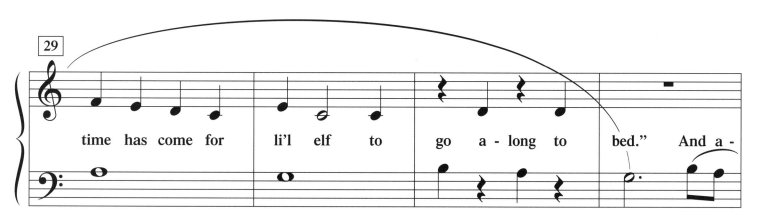

time has come for li'l elf to go a - long to bed." And a -

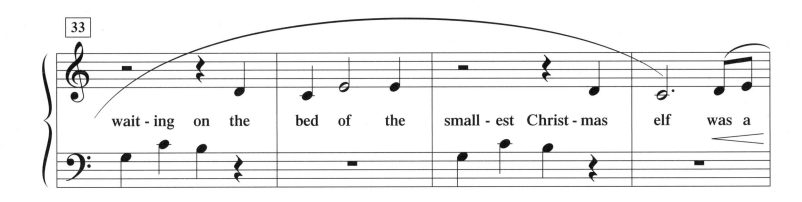

wait - ing on the | bed of the | small - est Christ - mas | elf was a

brown and cud - dly | fuz - zy bear from__ | San - ta Claus him - self!

mf

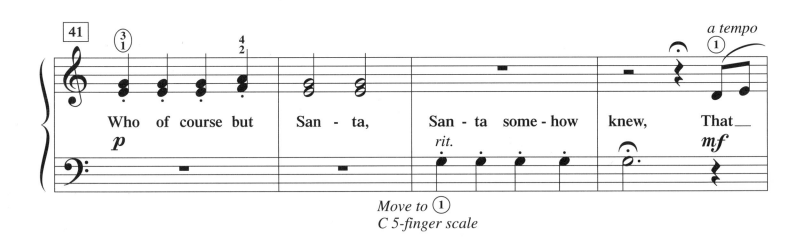

Who of course but | San - ta, | San - ta some - how | knew, | That__

p *rit.* *a tempo* *mf*

Move to ①
C 5-finger scale

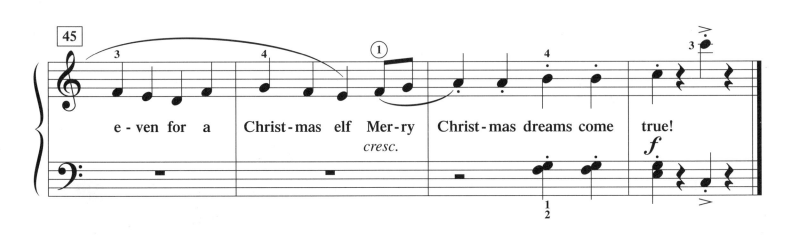

e - ven for a | Christ - mas elf Mer - ry | Christ - mas dreams come | true!

cresc. *f*